W9-DEZ-016

WILD AMERICA

TOADS

By Lee Jacobs

BLACKBIRCH®
PRESS

THOMSON

GALE

San Diego • Detroit • New York • San Francisco • Cleveland • New Haven, Conn. • Waterville, Maine • London • Munich

THOMSON

GALE

For Jake

© 2002 by Blackbirch Press™. Blackbirch Press™ is an imprint of The Gale Group, Inc., a division of Thomson Learning, Inc.

Blackbirch Press™ and Thomson Learning™ are trademarks used herein under license.

For more information, contact
The Gale Group, Inc.
27500 Drake Rd.
Farmington Hills, MI 48331-3535
Or you can visit our Internet site at http://www.gale.com

Photo Credits: Cover © Thomas Kitchin & Victoria Hurst; back cover © PhotoDisc; pages 3, 4, 9, 14, 15, 16, 21 © Corel Corporation; pages 5, 10, 11 © Joyce Gross Photography; page 5 © John H. Tashjian, CalAcademy Special Collections, California Academy of Sciences; page 6 © Alan Resetar; pages 7, 8, 12-13, 17, 22-23 © CORBIS; pages 8, 16, 17, 18 © John White; page 19 © PhotoResearchers; page 20 © Robert Byrnes

LIBRARY OF CONGRESS CATALOGING-IN-PUBLICATION DATA

Jacobs, Lee.
  Toads / by Lee Jacobs.
    v. cm. — (Wild America)
  Contents: The toad's environment — The toad body — Social life — The mating game — Toads and humans.
  ISBN 1-56711-646-9 (hardback : alk. paper)
  1. Toads — Juvenile literature. [1. Toads.] I. Title.
  QL668.E227 J34 2003
  597.8'7—dc21
                        2002003381

Printed in China
10 9 8 7 6 5 4 3 2 1

Contents

Introduction

In the animal kingdom, there are about 3,500 species of frogs and 300 species of toads. Frogs and toads are both amphibians. This means that they can live both on land and in the water. Amphibians are cold-blooded animals. Warm-blooded animals, such as humans and other mammals, have a steady body temperature. The body temperature of a cold-blooded animal changes with its environment. When the air around it is cold, its body temperature goes down. When the air around it is warm, its body temperature goes up.

Toads are amphibians. They can live on land or in water.

Because frogs and toads are so closely related, people often confuse them. They are actually two different animals. There are several ways to tell frogs and toads apart. Frogs have smooth, moist skin while toads have rough, dry skin. Frogs have long hind legs that allow them to jump high. The hind legs of a toad are short and are better for walking and hopping. Frogs have webbed feet and toads do not. Frogs have teeth and toads do not. And frogs must spend a lot of time in the water. Toads can be found far from a water source and do not depend on water nearly as much.

Toads live all over the world, on every continent except Antarctica. They are found in all parts of North America. Several toad species are common throughout the United States and Canada.

Toads have rough, dry skin.

Toads have shorter legs than frogs.

The Toad's Environment

Toads live in all kinds of places. Some toads burrow into the ground. Some live in trees. Others live along the shores of rivers or lakes. Toads can live in suburban neighborhoods, city parks, forests, marshes, mountains, and deserts. A toad might be found almost anywhere!

Swamps and wetlands are some of the many habitats in which toads live.

In warmer areas, toads will stay cool by burrowing or crawling into logs or other shelters.

Toads that live in cold climates hibernate. That means they sleep through the winter months. Many cold-blooded animals hibernate to survive the cold. Toads will burrow up to 12 inches (30 cm) deep into the ground. A toad's breathing, blood circulation, and digestion slow down during hibernation.

Toads that live in the desert do not hibernate. But they do cope with the extreme heat in a way that is similar to hibernation. They burrow deep into cool mud, and their bodily functions slow down. This kind of summer sleep is called "estivation."

The Toad Body

Toads have stocky bodies that range from 1 to 10 inches (2.5 to 25 cm) in length. Females are usually larger than males. Toads are often shades of brown, gray, or green. Some species have more brightly colored markings. In those species, females generally have more colors and patterns than males. Many toads have wartlike bumps on their skin. These bumps are called tubercles. It is not true that humans can get warts by touching a toad.

Below left: The toad body is generally short and stocky. **Below:** Females often have more colorful markings than males.
Opposite: Large eyes give toads excellent vision.

Toads have excellent vision. A toad's eyes stick out and are wide apart on its face. This helps a toad see in all directions. It can even spot something behind or above it! Toads have two eyelids like other animals. But they also have a third, clear eyelid that they can see through. This eyelid covers and protects the toad's eyes when it is underwater.

A toad's ears are called "tympana." A tympanum is different from most ears because there is no opening and it does not stick out. A tympanum works like a drum. Sound waves bounce off the tympanum's thinly stretched skin. This makes the skin vibrate, and the toad feels the vibration. A tympanum looks like a circle of skin on the side of a toad's head.

The circle of skin just behind the eye is the toad's tympanum.

Toad bodies are well camouflaged in their surroundings. **Inset:** Toads come in all sizes. This American toad is about the size of a quarter.

Social Life

Toads do not live in groups. There are certain times, however, when people may see large numbers of toads together. In hot, dry regions, toads burrow into the ground for protection from the heat. After a heavy rain, they come to the surface in huge numbers to soak up water. During mating season, a group of males may gather near a water source and sing to attract mates.

Toads use their voices to communicate. A male toad will croak loudly to find a mate. In general, males are louder than females.

Toads use vocal calls to communicate with one another.

Different species of toads have their own sounds. Some croak, some hum, and others make a trilling sound. Toads make their different sounds with a voice sac in their throat. The sac is made of skin that stretches out like a balloon, as it fills with air. The air that fills a toad's voice sac bounces off the animal's vocal chords and makes a croaking sound.

Hunters and Raiders

Toads are carnivores, or meat-eaters. They are also nocturnal animals. This means that they hunt for food at night and sleep much of the day. Toads will eat almost as often as they can find food. Adults eat a wide variety of insects, worms, snails, and small rodents such as mice and rats. While a toad is a young tadpole, it eats mostly plants.

A toad's excellent vision helps it find food. Toads also use their sharp sense of hearing while they hunt. A toad will sit completely still and look as if it does not see its prey (an animal hunted for food). When the prey passes near enough, the toad springs into action. A long, sticky tongue shoots out and snatches the prey!

Left and below: Toads are carnivores, or meat-eaters. They swallow their prey whole.

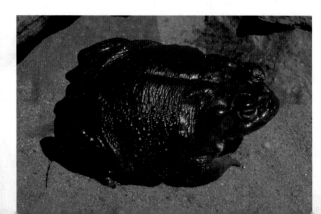

14

Toads protect themselves from predators (animals that hunt other animals for food) in many ways. When a toad is being hunted, it will often stand frozen in place. Some types of toads can scare a predator by puffing up their bodies to appear larger. Many toads have excellent camouflage. Camouflage is coloring that helps them blend into their surroundings. The ability to stay still while blending into the surroundings helps toads avoid enemies.

Toads also have a useful weapon of defense. They have two glands near their shoulders that produce a poison. A toad's warts also contain some of this poison. The poison will irritate most animals on contact. Animals that eat a toad will usually get sick. Only a few animals, such as skunks, raccoons, and garter snakes, are not bothered by toad poison. The Colorado River toad is one of the most poisonous toads in North America.

Poison glands in their skin help to protect toads from enemies.

The Mating Game

Toads do not interact much with each other until mating season. The timing of mating season depends upon the species and the area of the country in which the species lives. In northern parts of the United States, toads typically breed once a year, in the spring. In southern regions, toads may breed several times a year. In dry areas such as the Southwest, mating occurs only after enough rain has fallen to collect in pools.

Rain is necessary for mating because females lay their eggs in the water.

When toads are ready to mate, a male may travel up to 1 mile (1.6 km) in search of a water source. He begins to call for a female partner. A toad will sing loudly until a female that is ready to mate approaches him. Many toads singing together are called a breeding chorus.

The mating process for toads is called amplexus. A male toad climbs onto the back of a female and holds on until she releases her eggs, or spawn, into the water. Female toads lay eggs in two long strands surrounded by a jelly-like substance. Each strand can be more than 4 feet (1.2 m) long and contain several thousand eggs. The male then fertilizes the eggs with sperm. Predators will eat many of the eggs. A few hundred will hatch in the water within 3 to 12 days.

Left: A male's vocal sac will fill with air in order to produce a loud mating call.
Inset: Males and females typically come together only during mating season.

Top: Male toads climb on females.
Above: Some females, such as this Midwife Toad, carry fertilized eggs with them on their backs.

17

Tadpoles

By the time the eggs have hatched, each has developed into a tiny black animal called a tadpole. Unlike adult toads, tadpoles cannot survive on land. Tadpoles breathe underwater through gills. Instead of legs, a tadpole has a long tail that helps it swim. Tadpoles mainly eat algae and dead insects.

As tadpoles, young toads can only survive in water.

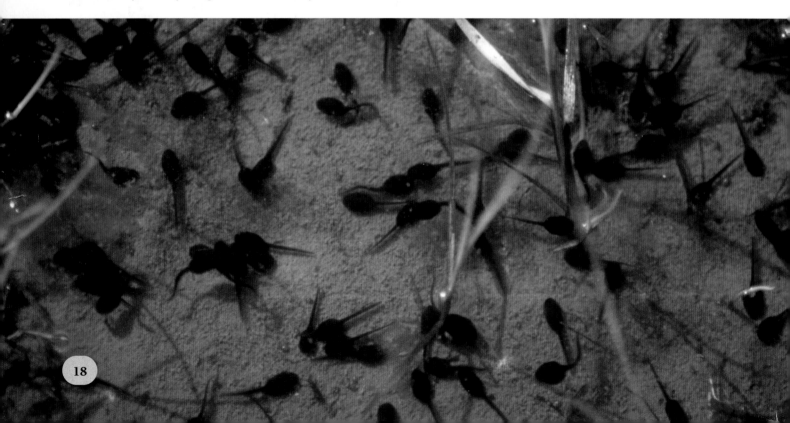

About 3 weeks after it hatches, a tadpole begins to change into an adult toad. This change is called metamorphosis. Within 3 to 5 weeks, a tadpole begins to grow legs. It also begins to lose its gills and develop lungs for breathing out of the water. Over the next 4 to 5 weeks, its legs grow longer and its tail gets shorter and shorter.

Right and below: To become adults, tadpoles grow legs and develop lungs for breathing on land.

Within about 10 weeks, a tadpole's tail is completely gone. Once a tadpole has fully developed into a toad, it climbs out of the water and begins its life on land.

Adults end up looking very different from when they were born.

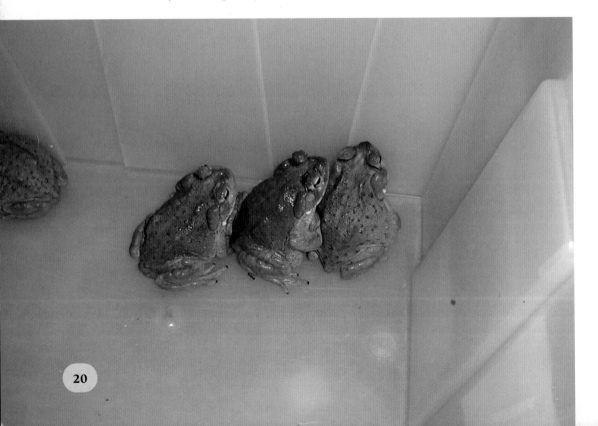

Most of an adult toad's life is spent on land.

Toads and Humans

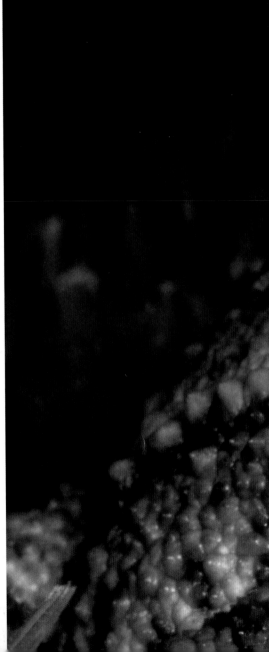

Toads are helpful to humans because they keep insect populations down. That is why many people are happy to have toads living in their backyards. One toad can eat thousands of bugs a month! This natural pest control also helps farmers protect their crops.

Many people like to find amphibians and keep them as pets. Kids may catch tadpoles in ponds and streams and place them in home aquariums. This can be an interesting way to learn about the changes that take place in amphibians. Once a tadpole becomes a toad, however, it is best to take it back to where it came from and release it into the wild.

Toads are generally helpful to humans because they help to keep insect populations under control.

Glossary

amphibian a cold-blooded animal that lives both on land and in the water

amplexus the mating process of frogs and toads

breeding chorus a group of male frogs or toads singing their mating call

camouflage any behavior or appearance that helps disguise an animal in its environment

carnivore an animal that mainly eats meat

estivate to rest during hot weather and allow the body to cool down

hibernate to sleep through the winter

metamorphosis the physical changes that transform an egg to a tadpole to an adult amphibian

nocturnal an animal that sleeps during the day and is active at night

predator an animal that hunts other animals for food

prey an animal that is hunted by another animal

spawn eggs

tadpole the organism that hatches from a frog or toad egg

tubercles bumpy markings on a toad's skin

tympanum the ears of a frog or toad

Further Reading

Books

Fowler, Allan. *Frogs and Toads and Tadpoles, Too!* (Rookie Read-About Science). Chicago, IL: Childrens Press, 1994.

Merrick, Patrick. *Toads* (Naturebooks). Chanhassen, MN: Child's World, 1999.

Miller, Sara Swan. *Frogs and Toads: The Leggy Leapers* (Animals in Order). Danbury, CT: Franklin Watts, 2000.

Pascoe, Elaine. *Tadpoles* (Nature Close-Up). San Diego: Blackbirch Press, 1999.

Index